Enjoy this lovely book
Louise Dickins.

Contents

Introduction

French style. Wherever I travel in France, I always
come across unusual objects and fresh decorating ideas
that bring together a harmonious blend of old-world
charm and crisp modern style. Creative details such as
a trompe-l'oeil wall mural, a damask upholstered chaise
lounge, or a simple row of ocean-polished stones are all
that's needed to add a special richness to any interior. I
have been collecting antiques and decorative objects for
years, crisscrossing the country in search of one item or
another. In the course of my travels, I have sought out
places to stay where a unique interior design style takes
center stage. I found that the French *maison d'hôte*,
or guesthouse, offers something special.

Today's guesthouses increasingly offer the comfort
and convenience of hotels but add the incomparable boon
of individual style and personalized hospitality. After
all, the goal of the successful guesthouse is to give the
traveler the impression that he is in his own home-away-
from-home ... but better, because the hosts who run it will
do all they can to ensure that the visit is exceptional. In
addition to a spacious suite or a cozy bedroom, a bubble
bath or an open shower, a special space for meditation or
a well-stocked library, a sunny terrace or a hammock to

laze in, you may well have the option of a thoughtfully prepared, home-cooked dinner. Plus you will be granted immediate access to a distinctive interior-decorating style and may even pick up ideas for making the most out of life, as simple to replicate as keeping a stock of flip-flops in a basket by your bath, hot tub, or pool. In the best guesthouses, you find your bearings and yet feel transported.

Those seeking inspiration for their own home interiors will find the guesthouses in this book rich in ideas suited to a wide variety of styles—elegant crystal chandeliers may be featured in one room, but a simple wooden bench, worn smooth with centuries of use, can be just as captivating in another. Gently faded neutrals create a quiet harmony in one setting, while another is alive with splashes of vivid color. Sleek and modern or cozy and rustic, each of these hand-picked settings is as inviting as a deep leather armchair.

The owners of the guesthouses described here have played upon the individual history, location, natural environment, and architecture of their house to create an environment that is as unique as it is inviting. For these guesthouse owners, the interior and exterior decoration

of their houses is a project close to their hearts—as well
it need be, for design has become an important factor
in our choice of where to spend our precious free time.
Travelers appreciate the clever incorporation of bona-fide
contemporary artwork, terracotta tiles, or hand-wrought
garden furniture into their vacation environment as well
as they do the independence and privacy of a room with
a view. They relish a surprising encounter. In this book,
the choice is wide: from a stylish room at a château to a
family suite specially created at a farm, from a building
that's been entirely converted to accommodate guests
to outbuildings patiently restored for visitors seeking a
bucolic getaway. There are former aristocratic residences,
shepherd's shelters, country houses and houses at the
water's edge, houses in towns and in small villages.
But all the guesthouses that I've included within these
pages have one essential element in common. They have
been carefully crafted by their owners to epitomize the
best of French style today and to show off the best of
France's art of living. As a result, you'll find yourself
able to use the book both as a guide for places to stay
when traveling to France, but also as a rich source of
inspiration for creating your own special look at home.

HISTORICAL HOMES

Each guesthouse has its own story to tell.

Some plunge their visitors into another time.

Cabalus

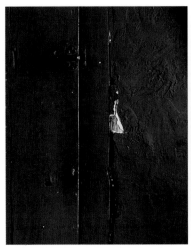

Rue St-Pierre / 89450 Vézelay
www.cabalus.com
+33 3 86 33 20 66

The village of Vézelay, a UNESCO World Heritage site,
is perched on the foothills of the Morvan nature reserve.
A visit here is a living lesson in history. The village's
basilica, a masterpiece of Roman art above the Cure
Valley, was once a rallying point for pilgrims, and it's
easy to imagine the little town buzzing with excitement as
a crowd of the faithful set out for Santiago de Compostela.
Hospitality is a long-rooted tradition in Vézelay.

Under the vaults of what once comprised the hostelry
and infirmary of the twelfth-century abbey, the couple
that own Cabalus house their guests in an atmosphere
seemingly beyond time. It was a crazy proposal
that brought this couple here from Switzerland in
1986, and they became some of the first pioneers
in the guesthouse adventure, when they broke with
their previous life to take over this spellbinding
building. Over the years, they have left their own
mark on it with restorations and renovations, all the
while respecting the building's rich past and unique
ambience. Their special genius? For combining
simplicity—of the medieval, monastic type—with the
jovial fantasy of their artistic whimsy. With its café-
cum-gallery, their house has become a living work of
art that defies classification. It's a place you promise
to return to even as you are leaving, launching a new
cycle of pilgrimage in this little town.

L'Hôtel d'Alfonce

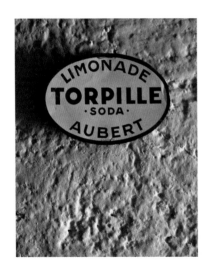

32, rue Conti / 34120 Pézenas
www.hoteldalfonce.com
+33 4 67 90 71 89

Make no mistake: Alfonce is not a hotel, but what in France is called a *hôtel particulier*, or an aristocratic town residence—and a very special one at that. The stories that owner Corinne Aubert tells bring added grandeur to the edifice. Built in the seventeenth century, with outstanding features such as a loggia, a spiral staircase, and an imposing Italian Renaissance façade that looks onto a courtyard shielded from the hubbub of the town, the *hôtel* once harbored the escapades of the court of the Prince of Conti. The famed French playwright Molière performed his first plays here for the Contis, at the start of his brief but brilliant career. In homage to the theatrical past of the building and to the notable guests it once hosted, Corinne, who is also a clothing and costume designer, has given a dramatic feel to her house: polished concrete floors, some high walls plastered

French Style
at Home

French Style
at Home

Inspiration from
Charming Destinations

Sébastien Siraudeau

Flammarion

with others left in their original state. On one living-room wall you can still see the flakes of former paintwork. The overall sobriety is broken by two tall trompe l'oeil hangings, unearthed at one of the antique shops in Pézenas, that could be straight from a theater set. The two hangings lead to the hallway and

the cool, attractive garden. In the
midst of this uncluttered decor, the
owner has scattered a collection
of old glass bottles with porcelain
stoppers. This takes us to the other
aspect of Alfonce's history. Jules
Aubert, Corinne's ancestor, bought
the residence, on credit, in 1883
and set up his lemonade factory
inside it. It was only in 1974 that
the *hôtel particulier*, now emptied
of its soda drinks, reverted to a
residence. After major renovations,
Corinne has given it a new life
with the authentic atmosphere
of a family home.

COUNTRY HOUSES

A guesthouse is like an ephemeral
secondary home, an ideal pied-à-terre
for a vacation in the countryside.

Le 33 (Le Trente-trois)

33, rue de Gournay / 60390 Auteuil

letrentetrois.free.fr

+33 3 44 81 94 90

Trente-trois. Thirty-three. At the risk of stating the obvious, "3" is a fetish figure at this guesthouse. So many owners of guesthouses have decided to leave their former lives to start over again. Naturally, Florence, owner of Le 33, has had three other lives. Her first belongs to the past: a career in Paris, small children, and a family house in L'Isle Adam north of the french capital. Already a desire for country life was beginning to reveal itself. Near her home, Van Gogh's

landscapes of Auvers-sur-Oise, the forests and valleys of the Vexin area, beloved to Monet, and the verdure of the Picardy area tipped the country-city scales and led her to her second life: running an old, country hotel that had cast its spell on her. In (three) waves of a trowel and with a palette of tricks, it was transformed into a guesthouse—the guesthouse Florence had been dreaming of owning. Because she loved traveling; because, above all, she loved design, her own design. Inspired by a mélange of Gustavian style from Sweden, Flemish colors, and universal design pieces, plus her own insatiable desire to collect and display.... As time-consuming as this is, she still finds time for a third life, one she leads under the blogger name of "Goumy." Thanks to Goumy, Florence can always be in two places at once, running the guesthouse while writing a chronicle of the everyday events of her life, and her decorating ideas and advice.

Le Canard à Trois Pattes

Le Castanet / 24620 Tamnies
www.troispattes.com
+ 33 5 53 59 13 85

Only in the country can you come across a three-legged

duck or "*canard à trois pattes,*" this one, no ugly

duckling, landed in the heart of the Black Périgord region

of west-central France—"black," as in the black of

the truffles or the black oaks that grow in profusion

here—just a short distance from the famous Lascaux

Cave, renowned for its prehistoric rock paintings, and

the historic town of Sarlat. The origin of this

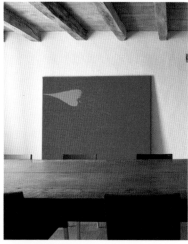

guesthouse's name—chosen by the highly creative brother-and-sister team from Antwerp, Helgi and Greet—remains a secret, but it's plain to see that, with their friend Armand, an artist and painter, they have fashioned something special from the authentic fifteenth-century farm they found in a state of utter ruin in 2000. Good interior decorators that they are

and experts with colors, they reconstructed the building stone by stone, using every single one of the bits and pieces they found on the property, including the increasingly rare, local *pisé* (rammed earth) stones that lay buried by time. When the work was completed with the help of a fourth accomplice, an architect, the main house had been returned to its original state: uneven stone floors, heavy doors, and local-slate roofing. To replace the outbuildings that were beyond restoring, they put up two cubes of wood and glass. The slim ensemble of buildings fits harmoniously into the surrounding countryside. Echoing the serenity outside, the interior design is markedly sober. Forceful materials—slate, granite, natural stone, and oak, and pure lines of minimalist furniture blend in with the wavy outlines of old beams. The purity is heightened by splashes of color both inside and out: bright paintings, and the blues and greens of the oh-so-bucolic countryside, belying the "black" of the French moniker for the region.

La Bergerie de Féline

Les Charles / 26460 Truinas
www.labergeriedefeline.com
+ 33 4 75 49 12 78

How many city dwellers have dreamed of moving to the country? And how many actually take the step? Brigitte and Jean-Jacques, born and brought up in the southwest of France, are of that rare breed. Before doing so, they embarked on an equally major adventure: a round-the-world catamaran trip with their six children. Once back on terra firma, they set their sights on a more pastoral environment, that of sheep and olive-tree

plantations, and weighed anchor in a green valley in the Drôme Provençale region of southeastern France. An old shepherd's barn nestled into a hillside became the focus of their new life on land. With the help of their families—decorators in the city of Lyon—they remodeled the building entirely, exposing the walls, scraping down the ceiling beams, and sawing blocks of wood. Their tireless efforts have transformed a rudimentary shelter into a welcoming country stopping place, where the authenticity of local materials harmonizes with the design of carefully selected furnishings. Guests who dine here will also get to catch a glimpse of Brigitte and Jean-Jacques's family life: personal black-and-white photos decorate the dining room. You will be able to share their memories of family, travel, and life in the country, while being nourished by the tranquil countryside, images of their children looking wondrous as they witness the birthing of lambs, and the organic bread baked by Joseph, who lives next door.

Un Cœur Très Nature

Place du Village / 30260 Liouc
www.uncœurtresnature.com
+33 4 66 77 43 12

This former silkworm-breeding establishment, tucked away in Liouc, one of the oldest hamlets in the Gard department in southern France, has been transformed into a cocoon of tranquility. Surrounded by natural scenery, this haven of peace is just a short drive away from major historical and cultural cities like Nîmes, Uzès, and Montpellier. With the help of her husband, Laetita has patiently restored the country house, transforming the

rooms into treasure troves
of carefully collected
birdcages, charmingly
timeworn pieces of
furniture, decorated
windowpanes, and as
many hearts scattered
around as your heart
could desire, to remind
you of the name of this
guesthouse, which means
"a very natural heart."
Laetitia has used the
gentle warmth of wood
and wicker to weave
the right atmosphere
for enjoying a complete
break, away from it all.
She does her utmost to
make sure you can follow
the instruction stenciled
on one wall: *REVER*.
Dream!

VILLAGE HOUSES

Take twisting streets that lead to a church square.

Unexpected havens of peace can be found

in the hearts of charming villages and hamlets.

La Maison Pujol

17, rue Frédéric-Mistral
11600 Conques-sur-Orbiel
www.lamaisonpujol.com
+33 4 68 26 98 18

A, B, C, D.... Let's start at the very beginning. La Maison Pujol has a penchant for the letters of the alphabet—made of zinc, wood, or plastic, or painted on canvas—used as simple works of art collected helter-skelter then displayed as if to convey a message. An old neon hotel sign, *AIMER* (love), displayed in capitals on the pebbles of the courtyard, reveals the essence of what Véronique, Philippe, and their children came seeking in this home hidden away in a little village in the wine-growing region of Aude. The thirty-something owners, tired of city life, following the example of a master sommelier, have managed to combine village and family life with running a guesthouse. This has not kept them from continuing their initial careers (one is an architect; the other a designer for a well-known brand). Their house is open for you to make

your own; the children run about,

only too happy to meet new friends.

For the Maison Pujol is a playful

place, not only for children, but

for adults as well. The minimalist

design in the bedrooms balances

perfectly with the easy-going

conversation at dinner under

the arbor, accompanied by wine from

the Carcassonne area—a natural

combination that makes

for the good things of life.

As simple as A, B, C.

La Maison

Place de l'Église / 30700 Blauzac
www.chambres-provence.com
+33 4 66 81 25 15

The south of France is thrilling: extravagant, exuberant, and eccentric all at once. But it also has a mysterious side, and this house, tucked away in one of those enchanting villages of the Gard in Provence, plays on this duality. The eighteenth-century building, located on the peaceful church square, only reveals its secrets to those who cross its threshold. Laid out at the foot of a hundred-year-old linden tree, its terrace garden

overlooks the Uzège
region. With its palm
trees, red wrought-iron
furniture, and pretty
table of potted plants,
it's a perfect place
for daydreaming. La
Maison knows how
to breathe deeply and
entices its occupants
to do so as well.
Its owners, Pierre
Berringer and Christian
Vaurie, have traveled
through Asia and the
Americas, and have
transmitted the spirit

of their voyages with subtlety throughout their house. After having run a guesthouse farther north in Touraine for seventeen years, Pierre entrusted a local interior designer, Richard Goullet, with enlivening his new spot in the sunny south. Lacquer paint and whitewash, pale blue and warm gold, azure floor tiles and stained cement—an entire palette of techniques complement Goullet's artistry. Adding his own creations to furniture discovered in antique shops and flea markets, the decorator has turned the house into a gleaming canvas that makes the most of the light and shadow of Provence. La Maison has been making its own little tour of the world in the press of late ... and has become a meeting place for travelers from the four corners of the earth. Its owners adore hosting all these people—though they still set aside a few months in winter to travel themselves.

Les Sardines
aux Yeux Bleus

Gattigues hamlet
30700 Aigaliers
www.les-sardines.com
+33 4 66 03 10 04

Charlie Chaplin singing in *Limelight* couldn't have wished for a better place to stay when he hoped to be reincarnated as a sardine: "Oh for the life of a sardine,/ That is the life for me." Anna used to be a model, Olivier a photographer. They met on a shoot, the years passed, and one day they decided to turn a page and start a family. In the sweet-smelling scrubland of southern France, the young couple came across an isolated village

with a crumbling seventeenth-century house that needed restoration from top to bottom. Using a good dose of elbow grease, augmented by knowledge gleaned from the entire collection of *Do-It-Yourself for Dummies*, Anna and Olivier set to work. After four years, the house sparkled, and they were ready to welcome guests. A majestic staircase leads to a charming terrace, which in turn leads to three cool and colorful bedrooms. Outside, there is a lovely arbor, a pool, and an additional discrete duplex. Inside, colors are warm, objects trawled from secondhand shops in the countryside add a bohemian note, and lovely old household linens are a final touch of luxury. Oh yes, we did find out where the "sardines" in the guesthouse's name come from: a locksmith left a stamp in the shape of a sardine on the door fittings of the house. What we don't know is why their eyes are blue....

FARMS
AND MILLS

Between field and river, cunningly
restored farms and mills have been
transformed into exceptional gems.

Le Moulin Brégeon

49490 Linières-Bouton
www.moulinbregeon.com
+33 2 41 82 30 54

The Industrial Revolution halted work at country mills, and their wheels and blades have long been motionless. The Brégeon mill, built in the nineteenth century, was a sleeping beauty left to go to ruin until the 1970s, when an artist came to awaken it. Jonathan Robinson, an American painter, calls himself an "artistic refugee." Fleeing city life and galleries, he set up his easel within a short distance of Angers and Saumur, between the woods and fields, the châteaux and streams, to pay homage to French culture and heritage. In partnership with two other people, one from Brittany and one from the Périgord, he undertook the renovation of the water mill to transform it into a guesthouse. To the authentic equipment of the mill—cranks, gears, and starting handles—he has added a motley collection of objects from the country and furniture trolled

from the flea
markets and bric-
a-brac stores
of the Anjou
area. Lopsided
candleholders,
enameled-iron
hanging lamps,
moss-covered logs
displayed like
sculptures, and
sassy black-and-
white portraits set
the tone for the
shabby-chic feel
of the water mill.
But a stay here

is not simply a trip to the country. For the three

partners offer thematic tasting tours in the Saumur

wine-producing area and French-cooking lessons

using products purchased at local markets, picked

in the organic vegetable garden, or freshly caught

from the river. These hands-on tours please not only

foreign tourists, there to get to know Brégeon and

its region, but also all the locals, grateful

to the threesome for having created a foundation to

preserve the local heritage sites. Even though

there is no longer a jolly miller to make bread

for the village, the site is just as invaluable

today as it was in the past.

Le Moulin Renaudiots

Chemin du Vieux-Moulin / 71400 Autun
www.moulinrenaudiots.com
+33 3 85 86 97 10

Here is yet another tale of a mill—but nothing outlandish.
It's just the simple story of Jan and Peter, who hail
from the Netherlands and Denmark. En route for the
long journey from their northern countries to the south
of France, they made a halt in Burgundy, stopping in
the Morvan region where, in Autun, they discovered
Renaudiots. It was as if this dilapidated ruin of a mill
with its garden run wild had been waiting for them to

come along and breathe new life into it. After three years
of hard work, the mill was transformed. The interior
seemed to have gained space, almost as though the pair
had pushed the walls outwards. The now-imposing living
room showcases fine, fluted stone columns, highlighted
by the workmanlike brushed-concrete flooring. The
combination of country and retro styles (particularly the
1950s Danish furnishing) creates a mood of tranquility.
Every detail bears the mark of careful attention: Peter,
who used to work as a designer, has a wonderful collection
of glasswork, displayed like something straight out of a
still life by Giorgio Morandi; Jan, formerly a nurse,
grows some of the produce he serves at dinner in his own
garden, *à la française*. The cuisine, just like the decor,
balances elements of Scandinavian tradition with typical
Burgundian dishes: poached eggs in red-wine sauce,
stewed escargots, scallops with pureed fennel, and
free-range chicken with freshwater crayfish and asparagus.
In short, you will find elegant simplicity in what has been
transformed into an enchanting environment.

La Ferme de Marie-Eugénie

225, allée de Chardenoux / 71500 Bruailles
www.lafermedemarieeugénie.fr
+33 3 85 74 81 84

At the eastern reaches of Burgundy lies the Bresse area. Somewhere between the towns of Chalon-sur-Saône and Lons-le-Saunier, the road disappears into the mist covering the apparently deserted countryside, so famous for the gastronomical-quality chickens raised there. At the end of an unpaved road lies La Ferme de Marie-Eugénie. For a long time, this family farm was occupied only on weekends and during vacations. Then Dominique and Marie-Eugénie

gave up their jobs in advertising in Paris to start anew in this remote country area. Dominique set to work, undertaking major remodeling of the outbuildings to transform them into guestrooms. Marie-Eugénie got going on the decoration, hunting down objects and furnishings, avidly reading magazines, and scouring professional fairs. Summer arrived, and the farm was ready to open its doors to visitors. The way to get there was properly signposted, and the first guests appeared—from Belgium, Switzerland, and all over France. The couple was somewhat surprised to discover that their remote spot had suddenly become a center of attraction—thanks to the internet, of course. But upon arrival, it's easy to see that there is nothing virtual about the charm of the place. What could be more real than the warm welcome that awaits you? The owners know the essentials of the good life. For starters, the cuisine is always generous: it includes, naturally, local chicken dishes, *jambon persillé* (the regional specialty of parsley-studded pressed ham), and a wonderful terrine that Marie-Eugénie always has in stock for unexpected guests.

CHÂTEAUX AND MANORS

Baroque, romantic, or medieval—
these places offer a chance to taste
the life of the nobility.

Le Château de Boissimon

49490 Linières-Bouton
www.chateaudeboissimon.com
+33 2 41 82 30 86

Welcome to the château. Its historical name is "Boissimon," but it's commonly known as "Linières," taking its nickname from the tiny Anjou village where it has always been the center of attention. Although not famous like its fellow châteaux of the Loire—Saumur, Chinon, and Angers—it shares much of their rich past. The Loire River, as is well known, has been far from a tranquil river. The first stones of Boissimon were laid in the thirteenth century, but the Hundred Year War erased all traces of the castle's far-off medieval past. Nothing remains of the fortified castle it probably once was; what we see today is an elegant Renaissance edifice dressed in limestone and topped with steep roofs of Angers gray slate. Each era and each owner has made a contribution: extending or transforming, and adding further chapters to its history. The last notable event took place in 1949, when

Prince Louis Napoléon Bonaparte held his wedding there. After that, for a long time, nothing of import happened, and the château seemed destined to decay. Then, at the turn of the twenty-first century, Chantal and Yves, in an anachronistic fairy tale, fell in love with it and decided to reawaken it. What was important to them was not so much its showy exterior, but the very essence of the place, an essence they felt impelled to share. And so, like true patrons of the arts, they worked with an interior decorator and a bevy of craftsmen and artists to give the château the finery it deserved. Stripped bare, all the rooms were given a new interpretation, from the floors to the ceilings, the colors to the materials, the furnishings to the smallest decorative objects, mixing Gustavian, Victorian, and contemporary design to create a new non-ostentatious sense of nobility. Of course, Boissimon is luxurious, but its new owners will welcome you with disarming simplicity, and tell you that the true heart of their château is, as in many ordinary homes, the kitchen.

Le Manoir de la Villeneuve

St-Aaron / 22400 Lamballe
www.chambresaumanoir.com
+33 2 96 50 86 32

There's no doubt about it; this is Brittany. At the end of the tree-lined drive next to the Villeneuve farm and its hydrangea-trimmed outbuilding stands a lofty manor with imposing granite walls. Their color is not the pink of the seaside town of Perros-Guirec, nor the gray of the Finistère region. Here, the stone hoists the colors of the Côtes d'Armor. The sea, its capes, the seaside resorts of Fréhel, Les Sables-d'Or, Erquy, and Le Val-André, and the distinctively Breton medieval towns of Moncontour and Dinan are a short distance away. Behind the seeming austerity of this eighteenth-century building, Nathalie Pérès has created a comfortable haven that is both calm and romantic. Gray wood trims, blue zinc, parquet flooring, damask fabrics, satin taffetas, chandeliers with pendants, embroidered sheets, and chuckling cherubs decorate the bedrooms, whose old-fashioned names—such as

"Rose et Céleste,"
"Mademoiselle," and
"Mignonne"—are
an invitation to put
time on hold. Or at
least to take the time
to make the most of
the tender colors of
Brittany as found in
the paintings of the
respected Breton artist
Mathurin Méheut,
whose canvases hang
at the nearby museum
of Lamballe. Or to
dip into the romantic
literature of the coast
in the books left
at their guests'
disposal in the
manor's drawing
room. Or simply
to enjoy the pleasure
of a leisurely cup
of tea by the fireside.

Le Château de Bordénéo

Bordénéo / 56360 Le Palais
www.chateau-bordeneo.fr
+33 2 97 31 80 77

With their ends-of-the-earth quality, as subject to
tempests as to sunny skies, the islands along the coast
of Brittany harbor reflections of surf and turf that can
be rough and austere. And, yet, a lovely château lies
hidden on the largest island, Belle Île (Beautiful Island).
This château, Bordénéo, is one of the island's most
discreet sources of pride. Belle Île—with its wild
coast, needle-shaped rocks known as the Aiguilles
de Port-Coton and an inspiration to Claude Monet,
northernmost Pointe des Poulains, delightful ports
of Sauzon and Le Palais, with its Vauban citadel—
sums up all of Brittany's generation and offers a
perfect condensed version of its history. The Celts,
the Romans, and the Normans all fought for it. The
Bretons evangelized it. Later, the British disputed its
ownership with the kingdom of France. It was only in
the nineteenth century that the situation quieted down,

and it became a destination for illustrious tourists, such as Monet and the actress Sarah Bernhardt. The Château de Bordénéo has been a silent witness to all these changes. In 1870, a Parisian began building a small château in the Italian style, all the rage at the time, on the foundations of a small farm run in the eighteenth century by an Irishman. He gave a very precise brief: a stone house, built over cellars, with a tile roof. There would be a first floor with seven rooms and two bathrooms. Above, there would be four bedrooms for the servants, an attic, and a storage room for fruit. A former mayor of Belle Île has written a well-documented historical account that describes the various owners of the château over the years, who ranged from a charity responsible for saving the shipwrecked to fortunate heirs. The current owners

have updated the building, turning
what were probably the servants'
rooms into stylish bedrooms for
their overnight guests. Since they
took over Bordénéo four years ago,
Françoise and Jean-Luc have made
this place and its history their own,
while breathing new life into it.
Although lucky enough to have
not needed to undertake any major
renovations, even discovering intact
an astonishing indoor swimming
pool of the Oriental style, they have
imbued it with their energy and flair.
The owners have recently renewed
their interior with fine new Loom
furniture and chairs to provide
a different ambience for future
seasons. Perhaps to be joined by
the latest works of one of the island's
many resident artists.

Le Château d'Uzer

Village / 07110 Uzer
www.chateau-uzer.com
+33 4 75 36 89 21

The Ardèche is a region of contrasts. Stark stony hills stand out on an arid horizon; the lush gorges for which this part of the world is famous tower above the blue Ardèche River. The road traces out a sinuous line, meandering through the spectacular scenery. Between Alès and Aubenas, it makes its way through the village of Uzer. All is calm; the village appears deserted. Although it may not have the charm of the neighboring

towns of Balazu and Labeaume, it is home to one of the most beautiful guesthouses in the region. And it's a château rather than a house, a genuine château, with a coat of arms, a keep, a guards' room, secret passages, and other surprises—a vaulted ceiling, and a suspended balcony, an exotic garden, and a lovely pool below. Its somewhat deconstructed solidity gives it a timeless quality yet, thanks to the talent, determination, and sheer spunk of the owners, it is also contemporary. And it took an awful lot of all this to get the château back on its feet again. Although Muriel and Éric had urban experience in the renovation business, working in the city was nothing like what they had to undertake in the country. With a tight budget, boundless inventiveness was required: recycling and creativity went hand in hand. The very ordinary Henri II chairs were reupholstered

with bright fabrics, transforming the dining room. Stones from the abandoned village train station were laid to border the swimming pool. Two caravans were brought to the far end of the garden and converted into stationary accommodations. Against the backdrop of the uneven château stones stands a miscellany of ultra-contemporary objects and pieces of furniture to update the ensemble. While Muriel prepares a generous cuisine of local specialties, Éric hammers away in his workshop at the latest piece of wood or iron he's found to make new garden furniture or another dining table.

HOUSES AT THE WATER'S EDGE

A small port, the banks of a river,
or an ocean view will start you dreaming
about voyages to distant places.

Le Clos Bourdet

50, rue Bourdet / 14600 Honfleur
www.leclosbourdet.com
+33 2 31 89 49 11

Fan and Jean-Claude Osmont were already well-known in
Honfleur. Anyone who went on an outing along the Grâce
Coast, for a walk around the docks, or a stroll in the
twisting streets of the small town invariably finished with
a stop for tea and cakes at their teashop, La Petite Chine.
After twenty-five years of running it, they decided
to make a change, settling in to another cozy place,
Le Clos Bourdet. The building, an eighteenth-century

manor house, has lofty views over the town of Honfleur but retains the warm friendliness that prevailed in their teashop, topped with a good dose of imagination. The notes of Éric Satie's melodies seem to float up from the piano in the living room. (Satie was born in Honfleur). The atmosphere is gentle, but the tone is quirky. Walls and wood are painted

in whimsical pastels—"seaside" blue, chocolate mauve, or soft yellow, depending on how the changing Normandy skies illuminate them. What is constant throughout the house is a marked taste for mixing and matching aesthetics and eccentricity: shiny chandeliers, panther fabrics, collections of unique objects hunted down in bric-a-brac stores, and, everywhere, Jean-Claude's large-format black-and-white photos. Even though they acknowledge that they owe something to places they've seen on their many voyages away from their home grounds—like the Villa Saint-Louis in Lourmarin in the Lubéron and the Comptoir d'Aubrac in Saint-Chély—Jean-Claude and Fan have made the Clos Bourdet a place unique to itself. And sure to please anyone seeking to relish the idyllic scenes of Honfleur that Monet once put onto canvas.

La Petite Fugue

9, quai du Foix / 41000 Blois
www.lapetitefugue.com
+33 2 54 78 42 95

This is a novel little tune that evokes the lapping of the
Loire River. When they hit forty, Michel and Michelle
decided to leave their careers in engineering and
marketing on the banks of the Seine behind them to set
up a home on the banks of the Loire. What they imagined
would be just temporary—they called it La Parenthèse
(The Parenthesis ... or Interlude)—left them anchored in
the city of Blois. After a few arpeggios, they started

Le Jardin Secret (The Secret Garden), an almost-private dining establishment for just fifteen people, with a hotel bedroom "just in case." The first few bars of their little fugue were already composed. After visiting no fewer than one-hundred-and-fifty houses, they finally unearthed their rare gem, nestling on the banks of the Loire. It is a distinguished house, with high ceilings and original parquet flooring.

The elegant decoration—cinnamon-colored linens and velvet throws—strikes just the right note.

A short walk from the center of Blois, the house is not far from the famous châteaux of Azay-le-Rideau and Amboise, the wine route and cellars of the Loire region, and the intriguing Petrified Caves of Savonnières. Michel and Michelle will give you expert advice on where to go in this fascinating region. They also know when it's time to unwind around their dining table, tying their aprons back on and composing delightful menus, replete with special recipes and gourmet surprises.

Ma Maison de Mer

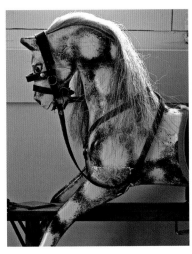  

21, avenue du Platin
17420 Saint-Palais-sur-Mer
www.mamaisondemer.com
+33 5 46 23 64 86

How many of us have dreamt of a life by the sea, sharing our time between the beach and the garden? Emma and Phillip Hutchison actually took the plunge. But for all that, they cannot be said to be on vacation all year round. They arrived from Yorkshire in 2004 to discover their house by the sea— which is what the name Ma Maison de Mer signifies—on what's known as the Coast of Beauty (la Côte de Beauté), near Royan. This house, which dates from the 1920s when

sea resorts were at the
height of fashion, is set
amidst pine trees just a
few minutes away from
the Conche des Platins.
It had initially been
a hotel—the very first
hotel in Saint-Palais-sur-
Mer—before it became
a guesthouse, ably run
by Emma and Phillip.
Even though they have
finished remodeling, they
have not stopped making
improvements. With
its white floorboards,
sea-rush mats, fine net
drapes, and lovely model
boats hunted down
in antique stores, this
guesthouse is almost like
being at sea, and just
what one seeks for an
ideal beach vacation.

Yamina Lodge

169, avenue de Bordeaux
33000 Cap Ferret
www.yamina-lodge.com
+33 6 14 69 36 80

Where in the world are we? In the tropics? On a Pacific
beach? No, this is the Atlantic coast, at the tip of Cap Ferret.
A fashionable destination as everyone knows; people
come to these parts for the soft sand, the pine trees, and the
view of the Bassin d'Arcachon. The next best thing to
owning a house here is a stay at Yamina Lodge. "Yamina" is
the name of the location recorded at the cadastral service.
Pascalou has been living in Ferret for twenty years now,

dividing her time between her seasonal openings and surfing the best waves of the planet. She's infused her lodge with a style that blends the surfing spirit with hints of Buddhism, adding the hippy-chic style of the Cap Ferret she loves so much. The lodge is made out of wood, some rooms left unpainted, some painted in the muted tones typical of the area. In addition to an entire villa available for rent by the week (its two bedrooms can be had on a nightly basis except during summer and annual vacation weeks such as Christmas and Easter), there are two completely independent bedrooms. Each has its own look: "La Divine" is immaculate white; "L'Exotica" is multi-colored. Natural objects—bamboo sticks, pine trunks, pebbles, and shells from nearby Sailfish Beach—meld into the décor. (The eponymous Le Sailfish is the area's trendy bar to see and be seen in during the summer.) Bicycles are available should you want to take a ride along the quiet streets. Alternatively, you can plunk yourself down on the private west-facing terrace, use the Jacuzzi should you feel so inclined, and enjoy the sunset.

L'Hôtel de Digoine

5, quai Madier-de-Montjou
07700 Bourg-Saint-Andéol
www.digoine.com
+33 4 75 54 61 07

Olivier Dutreil has traveled around quite a lot in Southeast Asia. In fact, his earlier life was centered on the Far East. But he decided to return to France and settle down finally, in the Rhône Valley. Digoine, in the village of Bourg-Saint-Andéol, seemed to have been waiting for him. This vast noble residence, once inhabited by an aging countess, was going to ruin. With Alix, his partner, Olivier undertook the task of getting it going again. He knew that

in the past the writers Musset, Stendhal, and George Sand had stayed overnight, and he could have taken these Romantic authors as inspiration for the interiors. Then, in the attic, he discovered the notebooks of a past owner who had been a silk merchant. This was the revelation Olivier needed for decorative inspiration. The rooms tell the story of the fabled silk roads that led from the banks of the Rhône to China. The homage to the previous owner, in other words, is told in shimmering, colorful silks that also reflect Olivier's past.

PROVENÇAL HOUSES

Where a local mas will charm you, and you can take
refuge in a bastide, soothed by the sweet-smelling
lavender and the special light of Provence.

K-ZA

Route du Moulin / 26790 Tulette
www.maison-hotes-k-za.com
+33 4 75 98 34 88

"K-za" is pronounced in French "ca-sa," as in the word for "house" in Spanish. And this is most definitely the house of Za ... Za being Anne-Elisabeth who, five years ago, left her kitchen in Metz in the east for a piece of Provence. The village of Tulette is located between the so-called Enclave des Papes (Papal Enclave) region and the northern part of the Vaucluse area. It proudly displays its motto: *Toustems libre* (always free). And this suits Za just perfectly, for here she has satisfied her craving for freedom. Her guesthouse was probably a bishop's residence or, more exactly, a residence granted to the bishop during the time—from 1309 to 1377—that nearby Avignon was the seat of the papacy. Avignon today has a major center for theater with an important drama festival, and K-za is having fun at last. Encircled by vineyards, the beautiful bastide is the ultimate in graphic design.

Black metal, rough concrete, and reflecting glass showcase the geometry of the old building. With just a touch of mathematics added in the names of the rooms: 1909, 8½, 3.14116, 69–96, and so on. Some sort of mysterious scientific calculation? No, you won't need your abacus. Not everyone knows exactly how high the Mont Ventoux is, which films Fellini made, what the value of pi is, or about palindromic numbers, but everyone can read between the lines and understand the art of living in this stylish house. Za is talkative, generously doling out her aphorisms, and is especially talented at enjoying life as it comes. She loves to share the hospitality of her land of plenty. Winter is the best season to enjoy the area. From November to March, Za organizes truffle weekends: there's a special menu, local wine auctions and, of course, the Provençal market and hunt for truffles in nearby Richeranches. With her yellow glasses perched on her nose and a green woolen bonnet, Za always sets off with a dried sausage in her right pocket and a piece of cheese in the left, prepared for the evening hour of aperitifs. By the close of the day, her guests also will have come full circle.

Justin de Provence

Chemin Mercadier
84100 Orange
www.justin-de-provence.com
+33 4 90 69 57 94

Eugénie and Victor, Thérésia and Marius, Augusta and Léon, Augustine and Achille, Marie-Jeanne and … Justin. No, this is not a list of the latest first names for babies in France. These typically Provençal names, each pair of which is given to one of the bedrooms in this guesthouse, are all of members of Isabelle's family. Justin was her grandfather, and he bought this stone shepherd's shelter in 1927. But he would barely recognize it now,

for Isabelle and Philippe, her husband, have imprinted their joyfulness and sunny natures—in short, all the characteristics of Provence—on the house. Justin de Provence, which lies languidly on the plain between the city of Orange with its famed Roman ruins and the steep lacy mountains known as Les Dentelles de Montmirail, embodies their love of interior decoration. Multicolored, patterned cement tiling and whitewashed walls are set off by an amazing collection of objects sourced at various antique and junk stores. Curios fill the house and spill over into the garden. There's an old bicycle with a basket and a wooden handle, a pile of old-fashioned enameled advertising signs, and more. The owners' generosity also overflows when it comes to well-being. In addition to the outdoor pool, much appreciated in this hot dry climate, the couple have just built one indoors. Created with an art-deco ambience, the new pool abuts a relaxation room, for unwinding in peace. It's an ideal place to lie with your loved one and dream about how to bring a taste of this lifestyle back home with you. Le Parfait Amour (Perfect Love) is the name of the bistro Philippe runs aside the guesthouse and opening onto its gardens, a scene worthy of one of the many Marcel Pagnol books and, later, films—such as *Jean de Florette* and *Manon des Sources*—set in the area.

La Maison sur la Sorgue

6, rue Rose-Goudard
84800 L'Isle-sur-la-Sorgue
www.lamaisonsurlasorgue.com
+33 4 90 20 74 86

Somewhat removed from the constant hustle and bustle of the antique market for which L'Isle-sur-la-Sorgue is so well-known, at number 6 on the rue Rose Goudard, a door opens on to one of the most elegant guesthouses of the town, an old aristocratic residence with several centuries of history behind it.

An enfilade of rooms leads to an immense living room paved in white stone, and this in turn opens on to a courtyard that has been transformed into an oasis of fresh air, complete with pool and an open-air dining and lounging area. The spaciousness of the rooms is enhanced by the skylight that illuminates each floor. Marie-Claire and Frédéric have lovingly restored or kept many of the elements of the past, such as the stone archway and the majestic staircase leading to the bedrooms. They have opted for a minimalist decoration that combines authentic

colors and materials, such as terracotta and varnished tiles from nearby Apt, with contemporary and ethnic touches. No doubt about it, their love for faraway places sets the tone of their house. When their guesthouse closes for the season, they take off. Their latest travels have included trips to Vietnam, Indonesia, and South Africa. They return with a bounty of souvenirs, dishes, objects for daily use, cushions, little pieces of furniture, and sculptures like the one they recently sourced in Bali. Their finds are on sale at the boutique just next to the house. Its name, most appropriately, is Retour de voyage (Back from Our Travels), and here they also exhibit the work of selected artists, both friends and those met in distant places, enabling their guests to leave with a tangible memory of their stay.

Les Rosées

238, chemin de Font-Neuve
06250 Mougins
www.lesrosees.com
+33 4 92 92 29 64

On the Riviera, everyone understands the language of luxury hotels, yachts, and private beaches. The language of flowers is less widely known. If you want to learn it, head in the direction of Mougins, above Cannes. At nine in the morning, the sun already floods the garden where the dew has barely dried. There is no mystery about the source of inspiration for the name Kilpérick Lobet has chosen for this guesthouse. *Les rosées* (morning

dewdrops) abound here. The house is a four-century-old Provençal building. There are a few suites for guests: Isadora, Saint Marguerite, Serguey, and Saint Honorat each have a salon or boudoir. As much attention is paid to your comfort as you would expect of a luxury boutique hotel, with bathrobes and fine bath accessories provided. But the spirit of the guesthouse remains artisanal, in the finest sense of the word, just like the work the owners put into decorating it. The muted, almost monastery-like atmosphere of certain rooms, with their rough walls, contrasts strikingly with the fine upholstery of the bed linens and drapes, all hand sewn in the family-run upholstery and interior-design studio next door, Les Ateliers de Mougins. One could live here as if one were on a Mediterranean island, far from the frivolities of the Riviera coast, appreciating the privacy the house affords. It's no surprise then that many of

the guests are couples getting away
from it all, celebrating a wedding
anniversary or on honeymoon.
And the souvenirs taken away
sometimes last forever—a young
English couple who came to enjoy
their last few days of freedom before
the birth of their baby actually left
with a little girl. Naturally enough,
they named her Eva ... Rose!

HOUSES
IN TOWN

Grand houses and aristocratic residences

are conducive to the enjoyment of a city.

Le Grand Duc

104, avenue de Condé
59800 Valenciennes
www.legrandduc.fr
+33 3 27 46 40 30

And now we're back in the city, starting off in Valenciennes, in the north of France. Granted, this may not be the spot that immediately springs to mind for a vacation—after all, most people are tempted to go south in search of the sun—but it is here that Philippe Collet decided to place his Grand Duc, meaning "grand duke," the name in French for the Great Horned Owl. As a young diplomat, Collet traveled from his native Lorraine region to Africa. But he put away both his former career and his suitcase in Anzin, where he bought the erstwhile home of a mining-company director. Directly across from the factory entrance, gates open up on a bona-fide bourgeois residence, typical of the north of France. A vintage Saab convertible faces aged red-brick walls. With a nod to the past, the owner has undertaken refined restoration work, with a serendipitous mixture

of modern style, gothic
touches, hints of baroque,
and a goodly dose
of contemporary art.
Collet is a visual artist,
an inveterate antique
hunter, a collector of
incongruous objects—toy
robots, Philippe Starck
dwarves, and rubber
toads—and ready to talk
about his passions,
including antique
shopping in Belgium and
enjoying the northern
region he's adopted. Just
part of why Le Grand Duc
has become the latest
must-stay guesthouse
near Brussels and Lille.

La Maison Bord'eaux

113, rue Albert-Barraud / 33000 Bordeaux
www.lamaisonbord-eaux.com
+33 5 56 44 00 45

Bordeaux, the elegant capital of France's Atlantic coastline, bubbles with excitement these days. Quays have been renovated, and entire neighborhoods transformed into pedestrian-only areas. The town is entering a new era. The Maison Bord'eaux is surfing on the wave of these changes and setting the trend for a new generation of urban guesthouses. Just a few minutes' walk from the heart of the city, this eighteenth-century,

former aristocratic
residence has a new
lease on life, thanks
to the initiative
of Brigitte Lurton,
a member of one of
Bordeaux's major
wine-producing
families. The owner has
introduced an audacious
snap of modernity into
this classic building,
using contemporary
materials and vivid
colors, and adding
touches of 1950s retro
style. This is a place to
be savored just as much
as the wonderful local
wines offered at
its small private bar.

La Maison Coste

40, rue Coste Rebouhl
11000 Carcassonne
www.maison-coste.com
+33 4 68 77 12 15

They were heading south from their native Poitiers and Toulouse, dreaming of Tahiti, but Michel and Emmanuel (better known as Manu), stopped north of the Pyrénées, on the banks of the Canal du Midi. The pair have weighed anchor in Carcassonne, and in the melting pot of this formerly Cathar city they've created their very own colorful island, a reflection of their Robinson-Crusoe ideal. While masses of tourists make their way

to the famous upper city, a UNESCO World Heritage
site, the Maison Coste remains tranquil down
in the lower city. Already, just a couple years after
its opening, it has become a favorite of those in the
know. First stop is a look in their boutique for some
delightful household object—which invariably leads
to a few minutes of rest and conversation in the
guesthouse's cozy tearoom. The guestrooms are
located on the upper floors, where the colors
and design ambience are decidedly Farrow & Ball,
the upscale British paint and wallpaper company, and
the mood is warm and cheerful. And, for those staying
over in Carcassone or at least spending the evening,
there are the dinners and special events like wine
tastings that they organize for New Year, Valentine's
Day, and other occasions—as well as the garden and
the Jacuzzi ... to which you walk in flip-flops that
have been thoughtfully left just for that purpose.

GALLERY HOUSES

Simultaneously gallery and guesthouse, these places bring a whole new meaning to the phrase "the art of hosting."

Le Domaine du Canalet

Avenue Joseph-Vallot / 34700 Lodève
www.domaineducanalet.com
+33 4 67 44 29 33

Household arts? At Le Canalet, art has taken over the house. Between the limestone plateau of Larzac with its harsh climate and the scrubland of the wine-producing Languedoc region, an imposing turn-of-the-twentieth-century house lies within a quiet green neighborhood in Lodève. Until Le Canalet was established, this small city's artistic fame was more industrially inclined; it was living off its past, when it was famous for the fabric it produced for troops and for its mines. But the construction of the highway and the famous Millau Viaduct, the tallest vehicular bridge in the world and a work of art in itself, was enough to decide a Parisian couple to settle here. Their project was singular: to establish an art gallery that would harbor a few guestrooms as well. After remodeling, the project took hold, offering guests the chance to stay in beautiful natural

surroundings within a museum of contemporary art.
As soon as you've climbed the steps, you'll find
yourself in the thick of things. A hoard of boars—
Hausey-Leplat sculptures wrapped in burlap—seems
to wander around the entrance. Your eye will be caught
by a mechanical movement: it's a zany automaton
designed by Michell and Jean-Pierre Hartmann,
the creators of the automated sculptures called
"Les Jouets de l'Imaginaire." Each room
in the house is an exhibition space. Senegal-inspired
furniture from the "Toubab" line, made with recycled
metal, and dreamlike paintings by Romain Simon
are everywhere to be seen. The trompe l'œil works
painted directly onto the walls are the only pieces
of art here that are not for sale! Everything
else is purchasable, with the sole exception,
perhaps, of the top-of-the-line Aga stove that
reigns over the guesthouse kitchen.

Chambre de Séjour avec Vue

Village / 84400 Saignon
www.chambreavecvue.com
+33 4 90 04 85 01

Here are the keys to the rooms in a guesthouse whose inspiration is in perpetual motion. Head for Saignon, a picture-perfect Lubéron village above Apt. More than just an artist's house, it's a place where art is an integral part of the décor. For over ten years, Kamila Régent and Pierre Jaccaud have been at the helm of this gallery, which serves equally as both an artist's residence and a guesthouse. The entrance of this lovely Provençal

home opens on a line-up of white drapes, an installation entitled *L'Isoloir* (The Voting Booth), which echoes the kind of booth the French use for elections. It's one of several works displayed in the hallways and living spaces. Because this is, indeed, a house where art has its place among the objects used for living. The bestial sculpture by Andrzej Wrona, peeping around one corner,

will testify to that. In one of the living rooms, a piano that once belonged to the writer André Gide stands side-by-side with an identical bronze miniature. In a hallway, tea is ready on a table but, look, there's a broken cup on the floor. Some hapless guest tries to pick it up, unaware that it is an ephemeral installation. A pair of pajamas hangs in the bathroom. There have been guests who, realizing that they had forgotten theirs, have actually worn these pajamas, only to learn the next day that they belonged to none other than Magritte. This is creativity at its height. It elicits a whole range of reactions and sometimes, even, dubiousness. Can one sit in the garden on one of the Tolix chairs with layers of paint in all the colors of the rainbow flaking off? Is this another work of art? Yes, indeed. These are the chairs on which you will sit for dinner. At Chambre de Séjour avec Vue (Room with a View), welcoming guests has attained a form of high art.

INSIDER'S ADDRESS BOOK

Following are the addresses of sixty-nine

guesthouses, which should guarantee that,

no matter which part of France interests you,

you'll be able to find an example of unique home

design and an experience of true hospitality.

Maisons d'hôtes

This list includes all the guesthouses shown in the book (they are the ones in bold), together with thirty-nine additional addresses. The price given corresponds to the lowest rate for one night in a double room with breakfast (which is usually but not always included in the room rate), though at some establishments rates may increase according to room and, especially, in high season. The price key is as follows:
€ less than 100 euros per night;
€ € less than 150 euros;
€ € € less than 200 euros;
€ € € € above 200 euros.
Consult the internet site of each guesthouse for more information.

Photo captions: p. 196: Lord Fred / p. 197: Les Fermes de Betty / p. 198: Le Clos Postel / pp. 200-201: La Maison du Moulin / p. 202: Le Corps de Garde / p. 204: Alegria, Maison Valvert, Chambres en Ville / p. 205: Au Ralenti du Lierre / p. 206: Les Buis

AQUITAINE & CHARENTES

LA BALANCINE
A charming house, typical of the Île de Ré.
3, Petite Rue du Marché
17410 St-Martin-de-Ré
www.labalancine.com
+33 5 46 35 04 04 / € €

LA BÉLIE
An authentic farm in the peaceful Périgord
L'Abeille / 24220 Meyrals
www.perigord-labelie.com
+33 5 53 59 55 82 / € €

LA CABANE DE POMME DE PIN
Seaside chalet
3, rue de la Brise / 33950 Lège-Cap-Ferret
lacabanedepommedepin.com
+33 6 77 35 44 50 / € € € €

LE CANARD À TROIS PATTES *p. 32*
Le Castanet / 24620 Tamnies
www.troispattes.com
+33 5 53 59 13 85 / € €

LE CORPS DE GARDE
House at the water's edge (photo p. 202)
1, quai Clemenceau
17410 St-Martin-de-Ré
www.lecorpsdegarde.com
+33 5 46 09 10 50 / € €

LE JARDIN D'HÉLYS
Family-run art foundation and guesthouse
Route départementale 705
24160 Saint-Médard-d'Excideuil
jardindhelys.free.fr
+33 5 53 52 78 78 / €

LA MAISON BORD'EAUX *p. 170*
113, rue Albert-Barraud / 33000 Bordeaux
www.lamaisonbord-eaux.com
+33 5 56 44 00 45 / € € €

MA MAISON DE MER *p. 128*
21, avenue du Platin
17420 Saint-Palais-sur-Mer
www.mamaisondemer.com
+33 5 46 23 64 86 / €

YAMINA LODGE *p. 132*
169, avenue de Bordeaux
33950 Lège-Cap-Ferret
www.yamina-lodge.com
+33 6 14 69 36 80 / € € €

BURGUNDY AND THE EAST

CABALUS *p. 12*
Rue St-Pierre / 89450 Vézelay
www.cabalus.com
+33 3 86 33 20 66 / €

LA FERME DE MARIE-EUGÉNIE *p. 84*
225, allée Chardenoux / 71500 Bruailles
www.lafermedemarieeugenie.fr
+33 3 85 74 81 84 / €

LA GRANGE À NICOLAS
Farm in the Jura region
5, rue St-Jean / 39290 Baume-les-Messieurs
www.lagrangeanicolas.com
+33 3 84 85 20 39 / €

LE MOULIN RENAUDIOTS *p. 78*
Chemin du Vieux-Moulin / 71400 Autun
www.moulinrenaudiots.com
+33 3 85 86 97 10 / €

BRITTANY

LE CHÂTEAU DE BORDÉNÉO *p. 102*
Bordénéo / 56360 Le Palais
www.chateau-bordeneo.fr
+33 2 97 31 80 77 / €€

LE CHÂTEAU DES TESNIÈRES
Elegant nineteenth-century château
Les Tesnières / 35370 Torcé
www.chateau-des-tesnieres.com
+33 2 99 49 65 02 / €€

LE CHÂTEAU DU PIN
Small château in the Breton countryside
Iffendic-près-Montfort / 35750 Iffendic
www.chateaudupin-bretagne.com
+33 2 99 09 34 05 / €€

L'ÉCOLE
*... a wooden seaside school you would never
play hooky from!*
2a, impasse de la Lande / 56520 Guidel
lecole.biz
+33 2 97 02 70 02 / €€

LES FERMES DE BETTY
Farm by the sea (photo p.197)
Le Stang / 29120 Combrit-Sainte-Marine
www.lesfermesdebetty.com
+33 2 98 51 99 14 / €

LES KORRIGANN'ÈS
An organic establishment by the sea
10, rue des Fontaines / 22260 Pontrieux
monsite.wanadoo.fr/korrigannes
+33 2 96 95 12 46 / €

LA MAISON DES ROCHERS
*A guesthouse where you can really
get away from it all*
65, rue Roger-Quiniou, St.-Guénolé
29760 Penmarc'h
monsite.orange.fr/maisondesrochers
+33 2 98 58 71 26 / €

LE MANOIR DE KERDANET
A faraway manor house
29100 Poullan-sur-Mer
www.manoirkerdanet.com
+33 2 98 74 59 03 / €

LE MANOIR DE LA VILLENEUVE *p. 96*
Saint-Aaron / 22400 Lamballe
www.chambresaumanoir.com
+33 2 96 50 86 32 / €

LANGUEDOC-ROUSSILLON

LES BUIS
*A manor house filled with an assortment
of antiques (photo p. 206)*
37, rue Carnot / 66130 Ille-sur-Têt
www.lesbuis.com
+33 4 68 84 27 67 / starting at 65 €

LE CHÂTEAU VALMY
Stylish, luxury, seaside château
12850 Argelès-sur-Mer
www.chateau-valmy.com
+33 4 68 81 25 70 / €€€

UN CŒUR TRÈS NATURE *p. 44*
Place du Village / 30260 Liouc
www.uncoeurtresnature.com
+33 4 66 77 43 12 / €

LA DEMEURE SAINT-LOUIS
An imposing house at the foot of the old city
2, rue Michel-Sabatier / 11000 Carcassonne
www.demeure-saint-louis.fr
+33 4 68 72 39 04 / €€

LE DOMAINE DU CANALET *p. 182*
Avenue Joseph-Vallot / 34700 Lodève
www.domaineducanalet.com
+33 4 67 44 29 33 / €€€€

L'HÔTEL D'ALFONCE *p. 18*
32, rue Conti / 34120 Pézenas
www.hoteldalfonce.com
+33 4 67 90 71 89 / €€

LA MAISON *p. 56*
Place de l'Église / 30700 Blauzac
www.chambres-provence.com
+33 4 66 81 25 15 / €€

LA MAISON COSTE *p. 174*
40, rue Coste-Rebouhl / 11000 Carcassonne
www.maison-coste.com
+33 4 68 77 12 15 / €

LA MAISON FELISA
*Traditional country house
with the latest in design*
6, rue des Barris
30126 St-Laurent-des-Arbres
www.maison-felisa.com
+33 4 66 39 99 84 / €€

LA MAISON PUJOL *p. 50*
17, rue Frédéric-Mistral
11600 Conques-sur-Orbiel
www.lamaisonpujol.com
+33 4 68 26 98 18 / €

LES SARDINES AUX YEUX BLEUS *p. 62*
Gattigues hamlet / 30700 Aigaliers
www.les-sardines.com
+33 4 66 03 10 04 / €

NORTH AND PICARDY

ALEX FACTORY
Outbuildings of a country manor
687, rue du Beaucamp
62720 Wierre-Effroy
www.alexfactory.com
+33 6 75 71 61 91 / €

CHAMBRES EN VILLE
Artist's house (photo p.204, bottom)
19, rue de Londres / 1050 Ixelles, Belgium
www.chambresenville.be
+ 32 2 512 92 90 / €

LE GRAND DUC *p. 166*
104, avenue de Condé / 59300 Valenciennes
www.legrandduc.fr
+33 3 27 46 40 30 / €€

LA MAISON CARRÉE
Spacious, artistic house in town
29, rue Bonte-Pollet / 59000 Lille
www.lamaisoncarree.fr
+33 3 20 93 60 42 / €€

LE TRENTE-TROIS *p. 26*
33, rue de Gournay / 60390 Auteuil
letrentetrois.free.fr
+33 3 44 81 94 90 / €

NORMANDY

AU GREY D'HONFLEUR
A small house typical of Honfleur
11, rue de la Bavole / 14600 Honfleur
www.augrey-honfleur.com
+33 2 31 89 55 20 / €€

LES CHAMBRES D'ANNIE
Trendy rooms with a sea view
10, rue Mouillère, Le GrandBec
14113 Villerville
www.leschambresdannie.com
+33 2 31 87 10 10 / €

LE CLOS BOURDET *p. 118*
50, rue Bourdet / 14600 Honfleur
www.leclosbourdet.com
+33 2 31 89 49 11 / €€

LE CLOS DES POMMIER
Elegant sea resort
5, rue de bas / 50560 Blainville-sur-Mer
www.leclosdespommiers.com
+33 2 33 45 03 30 / €€

LE CLOS POSTEL
Pretty seaside presbytery (photo p.198)
5-7, route d'Urville
50590 Regnéville-sur-Mer
www.clospostel.com
+33 2 33 07 12 38 / €

LORD FRED
Colorful country house (photo p. 196)
Le Lieu Robin / 14100 Le Mesnil Eudes
www.lordfred.fr
+33 2 31 63 87 13 / €

LA PETITE FOLIE
Oh-so-British residence in the heart of the town
44, Rue Haute / 14600 Honfleur
www.lapetitefolie-honfleur.com
+33 6 74 39 46 46 / €€

TOPOLINA
Great food and upbeat bedrooms
22, rue du Docteur-Couturier
14360 Trouville-sur-Mer
No website currently available
+33 6 24 55 14 32 / €€

THE LOIRE VALLEY

LE CHÂTEAU DE BOISSIMON *p. 90*
49490 Linières-Bouton
www.chateaudeboissimon.com
+33 2 41 82 30 86 / €€

LA GENTILHOMMIÈRE
DU BOIS-ADAM
Small country château
Le Bois Adam / 96, route du Soleil Levant
44450 Saint-Julien-de-Concelles
www.gentilhommiereduboisadam.fr
+33 2 40 13 10 00 / €

LA GUÉRANDIÈRE
Elegant townhouse within the medieval city
5, rue Vannetaise / 44350 Guérande Intra-Muros
www.guerande.fr
+33 2 40 62 17 15 / €

LE MOULIN BRÉGEON *p. 72*
49490 Linières-Bouton
www.moulinbregeon.com
+33 2 41 82 30 54 / €€€

LA PETITE FUGUE *p. 124*
9, quai du Foix / 41000 Blois
www.lapetitefugue.com
+33 2 54 78 42 95 / €

LA PINSONNIÈRE
An ecologically-minded house in Anjou
with an interest in world solidarity
225, rue du Château
49260 Sanzier Vaudelnay
www.la-pinsonniere.fr
+33 2 41 59 12 95 / €

LA TURCANE
Troglodytic house
4, ruelle de la Cour-du-Puits
49730 Turquant
www.la-turcane.fr
+33 2 41 38 37 44 / €

PROVENCE AND THE CÔTE D'AZUR

ALEGRIA
A really joyful house!
(photo p.204 top)
59, chemin du Stade / 83630 Aups
www.alegria.tk
+33 6 32 20 15 37 / €€

L'AUBE SAFRAN
Excellent dining at this Ventoux house
Chemin du Patifiage / 84330 Le Barroux
www.aube-safran.com
+33 4 90 62 66 91 / €€

AU RALENTI DU LIERRE
Large sculptor's home (photo p.205)
Village des Beaumettes / 84220 Gordes
rdlierre.free.fr
+33 4 90 72 39 22 / €

CHAMBRE DE SÉJOUR AVEC VUE *p.188*
Village / 84400 Saignon
www.chambreavecvue.com
+33 4 90 04 85 01 / €

JUSTIN DE PROVENCE *p.148*
Chemin Mercadier / 84100 Orange
www.justin-de-provence.com
+33 4 90 69 57 94 / €€

K-ZA *p.142*
Route du Moulin / 26790 Tulette
www.maison-hotes-k-za.com
+33 4 75 98 34 88 / €€

LE LIMAS
Stylish house in town
51, rue du Limas / 84000 Avignon
www.le-limas-avignon.com
+33 4 90 14 67 19 / €€

LUMANI
Artist's house in Avignon
37, rue du Rempart-St.-Lazare / 84000 Avignon
www.avignon-lumani.com
+33 4 90 82 94 11 / €

MAISON ROUGE
A completely natural house
Route de Nans
83640 Plan-d'Aups-Ste-Baume
www.mamaisonrouge.com
+33 4 42 62 58 92 / €

LA MAISON SUR LA SORGUE *p.154*
6, rue Rose-Goudard
84800 L'Isle-sur-la-Sorgue
www.lamaisonsurlasorgue.com
+33 4 90 20 74 86 / €€€€

LA MAISON VALVERT
Estate and cabana in the heart
of the Luberon (photo p.204, center)
Route de Marseille / 84480 Bonnieux
www.maisonvalvert.com
+33 4 90 75 61 71 / €€€

LES ROSÉES *p.158*
238, chemin de Font-Neuve / 06250 Mougins
www.lesrosees.com
+33 4 92 92 29 64 / €€€€

RHÔNE-ALPES

LA BERGERIE DE FÉLINE *p.40*
Les Charles / 26460 Truinas
www.labergeriedefeline.com
+33 4 75 49 12 78 / €€

LE CHÂTEAU D'UZER *p.108*
Village / 07110 Uzer
www.chateau-uzer.com
+33 4 75 36 89 21 / €€

L'HÔTEL DE DIGOINE *p.136*
5, quai Madier-de-Montjou
07700 Bourg-St-Andéol
www.digoine.com
+33 4 75 54 61 07 / €€

LA MAISON DU MOULIN
The perfect country mill (photo pp.200-201)
Petit Cordy / 26230 Grignan
www.maisondumoulin.com
+33 4 75 46 56 94 / €

Acknowledgments

To all the owners of the guesthouses
who opened their doors to me so I could
create this book.

To Ghislaine Bavoillot, Aurélie Sallandrouze,
Sylvie Ramaut, Kate Mascaro, Sophie Wise,
Tessa Anglin, and the rest of the Flammarion
team for their taste for good living.

To Farrow and Ball, and in particular to
Vanessa Coe, Beverly Collins, and Sébastien
Martin, for the visuals from the Silvergate
Papers collection, used at the start of each
chapter. Farrow & Ball Showrooms:
New York, Greenwich, Boston, Los Angeles,
Washington and Chicago +888 511 1121,
www.farrow-ball.com

To Gunnar Bellstedt and *Olympus France*,
www.olympus.fr

To the tourist offices, both regional and
local, for their welcome.

Aquitaine / www.tourisme-aquitaine.fr
Burgundy / www.crt-bourgogne.fr
Languedoc-Roussillon / www.sunfrance.com
Nord-Pas-de-Calais /
  www.crtnordpasdecalais.fr
Rhône-Alpes / www.rhonealpes-tourisme.com
  and www.rhonesalpes.tv
Riviera-Côte d'Azur / www.crt-riviera.fr
Provence / www.decouverte-paca.fr

Anjou / www.anjou-tourisme.com
Ardèche / www.ardeche-guide.com
Aude / www.aude-tourisme.com
Calvados / www.calvados-tourisme.com
Dordogne / www.dordogne-perigord.com
Drôme / www.ladrometourisme.com
Gard / www.tourismegard.com
Gironde / www.tourisme-gironde.com
Hérault / www.herault-tourisme.com
Manche / www.manchetourisme.com
Morbihan / www.morbihan.com
Orne / www.ornetourisme.com

and special thanks to Carole Bedou,
Sylvie Blin, Sophie Bougeard,
Cécile Broc, Sophie Brugerolles,
Sabine Canonica, Anne-Catherine Chareyre,
Isabelle Cholet, Nathalie Coupau,
Maryse Crumières, Alain Étienne,
Marie-Yvonne Holley, Armelle Jouan,
Catherine Jouffroy, Christine Kervadec,
Armelle Le Goff, Micheline Morissonneau,
Raphaëlle Nicaise, Patricia de Pouzilhac,
Hélène Ramsamy, Carole Rauber,
Blandine Thenet, and Gwenaëlle Towse.

To my family, friends, and all those who
enjoyed *Bord de Mer*, the *Carnets de charme*,
and *Vintage French Interiors*.

To Laure, Joseph, and Lucien,
my companions on all these photographic
journeys.

Translated from the French by Carmella Abramowitz Moreau

Editorial Director: Ghislaine Bavoillot

Design: Sébastien Siraudeau

Copyediting: Anne Korkeakivi

Typesetting: Olivier Canaveso

Proofreading: Fui Lee Luk

Color separation: Altavia Lille

All photographs were taken with the e-system.

OLYMPUS

Your Vision, Our Future

Distributed in North America by Rizzoli International Publications, Inc.

Originally published in French as *Maisons d'hôte*

© Flammarion, SA, Paris, 2008

English-language edition

© Flammarion, SA, Paris, 2009

editions.flammarion.com

10 11 12 4 3 2

ISBN: 978-2-0803-0084-3

Dépôt légal: 02/2009

Printed in Slovenia by Korotan